I0411026

**Future Direction of**

**U.S. NORTHERN COMMAND**

**AND**

**NORTH AMERICAN AEROSPACE DEFENSE COMMAND**

Chairman McKeon, Congressman Smith, distinguished members of the Committee, thank you for the opportunity to report on the posture and future direction of United States Northern Command (USNORTHCOM) and North American Aerospace Defense Command (NORAD). Our integrated staffs carry on a legacy of over 55 years of continental defense under NORAD, and USNORTHCOM's 11 years of safeguarding the homeland through innovative programs, robust partnerships, and continual improvement. The nation is well served by the commands' professionals who are focused on deterring, preventing, and if necessary, defeating threats to our security.

## INTRODUCTION

This is a time of dynamic unpredictability for the Department of Defense (DOD). As the world grows increasingly volatile and complex, threats to our national security are becoming more diffuse and less attributable. This evolution demands continuous innovation and transformation within the armed forces and the national security architecture. Meanwhile, fiscal constraints have further compelled us to rethink our strategies, reorient the force, rebalance risk across competing missions, and take uncommon actions to achieve spending reductions. Particularly troubling, in dealing with sequestration last year, we broke faith with our civilian workforce. Implementing furloughs as a cost-cutting measure compromised morale, unsettled families, and understandably caused many DOD civilians to reevaluate their commitment to civil service by undermining one of the most significant competitive advantages the DOD offers its civilian workforce, stability.

While we must deal realistically with limited budgets, the homeland must be appropriately resourced to protect our sovereignty, secure critical infrastructure, offer sanctuary to our citizens, and provide a secure base from which we project our national power. As a desired target of our adversaries, the homeland is increasingly vulnerable to an array of evolving threats. Thus, we should not give ground when it comes to defense of the nation and the protection of North America. USNORTHCOM and NORAD are priority investments in national security that should not be compromised as a consequence of the budget environment. When Canada was confronted with similar fiscal pressures to those encountered here, they fully resourced NORAD. Holding up our end of shared defense through NORAD honors Canada's commitment, and is a key element of our nation's competitive advantage across an uncertain global landscape.

The USNORTHCOM geographic area of responsibility encompasses North America. It includes the Gulf of Mexico, the Straits of Florida, much of the Caribbean region (U.S. Virgin Islands, British Virgin Islands, Bermuda, Puerto Rico, The Bahamas, and Turks and Caicos Islands), and the approaches to the continent, including significant portions of the Atlantic, Pacific, and Arctic Oceans.

Homeland defense depends on readiness and preparedness. The dedicated professionals from the Intelligence community, including the National Security Agency (NSA) and other organizations, provide vital indications and warnings enabling the continued security and defense of our nation. The recent and potential future compromises of intelligence information, including the capabilities of the NSA, an agency with which NORAD/USNORTHCOM relies on with an effective operational partnership, profoundly disrupts and impacts how we deter terrorists and defend the homeland.

Further, although I am encouraged by the short-term stability obtained by recent passage of the Bipartisan Budget Act of 2013, the shadow of sequestration still looms over key strategic decisions concerning how we defend the nation over the next two decades. Should sequestration return in 2016, it would lead to a situation where combat readiness and modernization could not fully support current and projected requirements to defend the homeland. Underinvestment in capabilities which sustain readiness increases our vulnerability and risk. The nation deserves better than a hollow force lacking the capability or capacity to confront threats.

> **My priorities:**
> * Expand and strengthen our trusted partnerships
> * Advance and sustain the bi-national military command
> * Gain and maintain all-domain situational awareness
> * Advocate and develop capabilities in our core mission areas to outpace all threats
> * Take care of our people; they are our foundation

Distinct from other geographic combatant commands, we must observe and comply with domestic legal and policy requirements as a condition of operating in the homeland. Under the direction of the President and Secretary of Defense, USNORTHCOM and NORAD deliver effective, timely DOD support to a wide variety of tasks in the homeland and ultimately defend our citizens and property from attack. Our commands work in an environment governed by domestic laws, and guided by the policies, traditions, and customs our country has developed over centuries in the use and roles of armed forces at home. We also hold the obligation of serving citizens with deservedly high expectations for decisive action from the military in times of need. In this environment, it is imperative we retain the ability to outpace threats and maintain all-domain situational awareness to allow greater decision space for strategic leaders. The commands' approach is to defend the homeland "forward" and in-depth through trusted partnerships with fellow combatant commands, our hemispheric neighbors, and the interagency community. We carry out our primary missions of homeland defense, security cooperation, and civil support with a focus on preparation, partnerships, and vigilance.

**HOMELAND DEFENSE**

USNORTHCOM and NORAD are part of a layered defense of the homeland designed to respond to threats before they reach our shores. Our national security architecture must be capable of deterring and defeating traditional and asymmetric threats including aircraft, ballistic missiles, terrorism, and cyber-attacks on economic systems and critical infrastructure. In the maritime domain, advances in submarine-launched cruise missiles and submarine technologies challenge our homeland defense efforts, as does our aging undersea surveillance infrastructure. Additionally, we recognize the Arctic as an approach to the homeland and must account for emerging concerns and opportunities related to greater accessibility and human activity in the region. We support the federal response to many threats facing the nation which are primarily security or law enforcement related, while ultimate responsibility for defending against and defeating direct attacks by state and non-state actors rests with DOD

> NORAD Mission: North American Aerospace Defense Command conducts aerospace warning, aerospace control, and maritime warning in the defense of North America.

### *Aerospace Warning and Control*

In the performance of our aerospace missions, including Operation NOBLE EAGLE, NORAD defends North American airspace and safeguards key national terrain by employing a combination of armed fighters, aerial refueling, Airborne Warning and Control System (AWACS) surveillance platforms, the National Capital Region Integrated Air Defense System, and ground-based Air Defense Sector surveillance detection capabilities. We regularly exercise our three NORAD Regions and USNORTHCOM Components through Exercise VIGILANT SHIELD.

Over the past year, we launched fighters, AWACS, and tankers from the Alaskan and Canadian NORAD Regions in response to Russian Long-Range Aviation. These sorties, as in the past, were not identified on international flight plans and penetrated the North American Air Defense Identification Zone. Detect and intercept operations demonstrated our ability and intent to defend the northern reaches of our homelands and contribute to our strategic deterrence of aerospace threats to the homeland.

NORAD regions are an integral part of our homeland defense mission. Their capability to provide mission-ready aircraft and pilots across all platforms plays a critical role in our common defense with Canada. The ability of NORAD to execute our primary mission is placed at significant risk given the degradation of U.S. Combat Air Force readiness, which hovers at 50 percent. The lack of ready forces is directly attributable to the fiscal pressure placed on readiness accounts and the subsequent challenges our Air Force Service Provider faces to execute modernization and recapitalization programs.

We are partnering with the Air Force to take decisive steps to restructure forces and regain readiness by innovatively making every training sortie count. However, I am concerned about our mid- and long-term capability to deliver the deterrent effects required of NORAD. If the Budget Control Act persists beyond fiscal year 2015, the extraordinary measures being undertaken by the Air Force to preserve readiness may not be enough to assure that combat forces can satisfy NORAD requirements. Reversing current negative readiness trends will require considerable time and expense to return squadrons to mission-ready status. For example, one of only two annual Air Force Weapons Instructor Courses, and two RED FLAG exercises, were cancelled this past year which will have an enduring impact on the readiness, training, and preparedness of our Air Force. Now more than ever, the Air Force's efforts to seek an appropriate balance between readiness today and tomorrow will have a key impact on NORAD's current and future success.

---

USNORTHCOM Mission: United States Northern Command partners to conduct homeland defense, security cooperation, and civil support, to defend and secure the United States and its interests.

---

*Missile Defense*

We remain vigilant to nations developing the capability to threaten our homeland with ballistic missiles. While tensions have subsided for the time being, North Korea continues to ignore United Nations resolutions and seeks international recognition as a nuclear-armed state, which we oppose. North Korea again showcased its new road-mobile Intercontinental Ballistic Missile (ICBM) during a military parade this past July. Similarly, while Iran does not yet possess a nuclear weapon and professes not to seek one, it is developing advanced missile capabilities faster than previously assessed. Iran has successfully orbited satellites, demonstrating technologies directly relevant to the development of an ICBM. Tangible evidence of North Korean and Iranian ambitions reinforces our understanding of how the ballistic missile threat to the homeland has matured from a theoretical to a practical consideration. Moreover, we are concerned about the potential for these lethal technologies to proliferate to other actors.

I remain confident in our current ability to defend the United States against ballistic missile threats from North Korea or Iran. However, advancing missile technologies demand improvement to the Ballistic Missile Defense System architecture in order to maintain our strategic advantage. We are working with the Missile Defense Agency (MDA) on a holistic approach to programmatically invest in tailored solutions. A steady-testing schedule and continued investment are needed to increase reliability and resilience across the missile defense enterprise. We are pursuing a more robust sensor architecture capable of providing kill assessment information and more reliable Ground-based Interceptors (GBIs). Additionally, we are deliberately assessing improvements to the nation's intelligence collection and surveillance capability in order to improve our understanding of adversary capability and intent. Finally, we recognize the proliferation of threats that will challenge BMD inventories. Over time, missile defense must become an integral part of new deterrence strategies towards rogue states that balance offensive as well as defensive capabilities.

In March 2013, the Secretary of Defense announced plans to strengthen homeland ballistic missile defense by increasing the number of GBIs from 30 to 44, and deploying a second TPY-2 radar to Japan. USNORTHCOM is actively working with our mission partners to see that these activities are completed as soon as possible. We are supporting MDA's study evaluating possible locations in the U.S., should we require an additional missile defense interceptor site. When required based upon maturity of the threat, a third site will enable greater weapons access, increased GBI inventory, and increased battlespace against threats, such as those from North Korea and Iran. Choosing a third site is dependent on numerous factors including battlespace geometry, sensors, command and control, and interceptor improvements. Finally, with the support of Congress, we are making plans for deployment of a new long-range discriminating radar and assessing options for future sensor architecture.

Our ability to detect, track and engage airborne threats, including emerging cruise missile technology, was the principal focus of our recently completed Defense Design for the National Capital Region. Next winter we will begin a three-year Joint Land Attack Cruise Missile Defense Elevated Netted Sensor (JLENS) operational exercise at Aberdeen Proving Ground, establishing a new capability to detect and engage cruise missiles at range before they threaten the Washington D.C. area. NORAD will combine JLENS capabilities with the Stateside Affordable Radar System into the existing air defense structure. These capabilities can point to a next generation air surveillance capability for homeland cruise missile defense.

*Maritime*

NORAD conducts its maritime warning mission on a global scale through an extensive network of information sharing on potential maritime threats to the U.S. and Canada. Our execution of this mission continues to mature—we issued 14 maritime warnings or advisories in 2013, six more than the previous year. Through USNORTHCOM's cooperative maritime defense, we gain and maintain situational awareness to detect, warn of, deter, and defeat threats within the domain.

In 2013, to improve capability and enhance homeland command and control relationships in the maritime domain, U.S. Fleet Forces Command was designated U.S. Naval Forces North, providing USNORTHCOM with an assigned naval component on the East Coast. We are also working in parallel with U.S. Pacific Command to close seams for command and control on the West Coast. These initiatives support DOD's strategic pivot to the Asia-Pacific and account for the increased pace of Russian and Chinese maritime activity in our Area of Responsibility (AOR), including their forays into the Arctic.

*NORAD Strategic Review*

Consistent with my priority to advance and sustain the bi-national military command, at the direction of the Chairman of the Joint Chiefs of Staff and Canada's Chief of the Defence Staff, we recently initiated a NORAD Strategic Review. The Review intends to capitalize on existing synergies and identify opportunities to evolve NORAD into an agile, modernized command capable of outpacing the full spectrum of threats. The review identified promising opportunities to improve operational effectiveness, several of which can be implemented immediately. For example, we can realize benefits from aligning the U.S. and Canadian readiness reporting processes and by collaborating closely on continental threat assessment and capability development processes.

## *The Arctic*

The Arctic, part of the NORAD area of operations and USNORTHCOM AOR, is historic key terrain for DOD in defense of North America. With decreasing seasonal ice, the Arctic is evolving into a true strategic approach to the homeland. Arctic and non-Arctic nations are updating their strategies and positions on the future of the region through a variety of international forums and observable activities. Russia, after decades of limited surface activity, significantly increased its naval operations in the high north. This activity included multi-ship exercises as well as an unprecedented amphibious landing and reestablishment of a long-closed airbase in the New Siberian Islands. Also, China recently achieved formal observer status on the Arctic Council; continues diplomatic, scientific, and trade initiatives with Nordic nations; and is making progress on a second polar icebreaker. While potential for friction exists, the opening of the Arctic presents an historic opportunity to solidify and expand strategic partnerships and cooperation.

We fulfill our responsibilities as the DOD's advocate for Arctic capabilities by working with stakeholders to develop military capabilities to protect U.S. economic interests, maritime safety, and freedom of maneuver. We prepare for attendant security and defense considerations should countries and commercial entities disagree over sea-transit routes and lucrative natural resources. Secretary Hagel's comments on this subject are pertinent, "Throughout human history, mankind has raced to discover the next frontier. And time after time, discovery was swiftly followed by conflict. We cannot erase this history. But we can assure that history does not repeat itself in the Arctic." To this end, we are pursuing advancements in communications, domain awareness, infrastructure, and presence to outpace the potential challenges that accompany increased human activity.

The Department's desired end state for the Arctic is a secure and stable region where U.S. national interests are safeguarded, the U.S. homeland is protected, and nations work cooperatively. With Canada as our premier partner in the Arctic, NORAD and USNORTHCOM seek to improve our bi-national and bi-lateral abilities to provide for defense, safety, security, and cooperative partnerships in the Arctic. To enhance these endeavors, I continue to support accession to the Law of the Sea Convention, which would give the U.S. a legitimate voice within the Convention's framework.

### *Exercises/Lessons Learned*

To ensure our readiness for homeland defense missions, we rely on a robust joint training and exercise program to develop and refine key capabilities. In the last two years, we incorporated other combatant command and multinational participation in our major exercises like VIGILANT SHIELD, which more closely approximates how we expect to respond to real-world contingencies or crises. An integrated approach also ensures we work in unison with our domestic and international partners to reinforce mutual response capabilities and sustain our ability to project power.

Additionally, USNORTHCOM and NORAD, while postured to respond to unwanted Russian aerospace activity, conducted a successful annual Air Control exercise with the armed forces of the Russian Federation. Known as VIGILANT EAGLE, this exercise simulated fighter aircraft from the U.S., Canada, and Russia working cooperatively to intercept a hijacked passenger aircraft traveling between the three nations. Once intercepted, we transferred control of the aircraft to Russia to escort the plane as it landed in their territory. This combined exercise expanded dialogue and cooperation, sustained defense contacts, and fostered understanding among our governments and militaries.

## SECURITY COOPERATION

Defending the homeland in depth requires partnership with our neighbors—Canada, Mexico, and The Bahamas—to confront shared security concerns and guard the approaches to the continent and the region.

The U.S.-Canada NORAD Agreement is the gold standard for cooperation between nations on common defense. Our security partnership with Canada has pushed out the protected perimeter of our homelands to the furthest extents of the continent. Their meaningful contributions to the defense of North America through NORAD, and globally through the North Atlantic Treaty Organization, make Canada an indispensable ally. Defending together is the principal competitive advantage we enjoy in defending our homelands.

In the rest of our AOR, theater security cooperation activities focus on being the defense partner of choice in working on common regional security issues. The proliferation and influence of Transnational Criminal Organizations (TCOs) pose social, economic, and security challenges for the U.S., Canada, Mexico, and The Bahamas. A related threat is the potential for Middle Eastern and other terrorist organizations to exploit pathways into the U.S. by using their increased presence in Latin America and exploiting the destabilizing influence of organized crime networks. Our efforts to counter transnational organized crime focus on providing support to our U.S. law enforcement partners, other U.S. government agencies, and our military partners in the AOR. Theater security cooperation activities involve detailed and collaborative planning with our partners' militaries and federal agencies. Throughout the process, we remain respectful of our partners' national sovereignty and frame our initiatives with that in mind.

*Canada*

In addition to ongoing activities in NORAD, our security cooperation with Canada includes all-domain awareness; regional partner engagement; cross-border mitigation support of chemical, biological, radiological, and nuclear incidents; and combined training and exercises. Over the past year, we began discussing cooperative efforts in cyber and concluded an action plan for further cooperation in the Arctic.

Last June, the Chairman of the Joint Chiefs of Staff hosted Canada's Chief of the Defence Staff in a first-ever Defense Chiefs Strategic Dialogue. The Chairman and Chief agreed to pursue several initiatives over the next year, including the NORAD Strategic Review, ongoing USNORTHCOM and NORAD cooperative efforts on regional engagement, cyber, and combined training; our relationship has never been stronger.

*Mexico*

A strong security relationship with Mexico is a critical strategic imperative reflecting the power of our shared economic, demographic, geographic, and democratic interests. An enduring partnership with a secure and prosperous Mexico is a necessary precondition to the long-term security and prosperity of the U.S. and the Western Hemisphere. Our nations share responsibility for disabling and dismantling the illicit criminal networks that traffic narcotics and other contraband into the U.S., and illegal weapons and illicit revenues into Mexico. TCOs continue to establish support zones, distribute narcotics, and conduct a wide variety of illicit activities within the U.S., corrupting our institutions, threatening our economic system, and compromising our security. International and interagency pressure on these networks is essential to reduce the threat posed to our citizens and allow for the strengthening of rule of law institutions for hemispheric partners.

At the request of the Government of Mexico, while being mindful of Mexican sovereignty, we partner with the Mexican Army (SEDENA) and Navy (SEMAR) on security issues of mutual interest. USNORTHCOM provides focused engagements, professional exchanges, military equipment, and related support that advance common goals. Our engagements further mutual trust, enhance collaboration, and increase mutual capability to counter transnational threats and meet our many common security concerns. Recent successes include QUICKDRAW, a tactical-level exercise that tested the capabilities of U.S., Canadian, and Mexican maritime forces in joint response to illicit activities; subject matter expert exchanges enabling participants to learn and refine best military practices; and bilateral and multilateral conferences achieving broader coordination on issues such as natural disasters, pandemics, and search and rescue.

USNORTHCOM continues to grow our relationship with SEDENA and SEMAR with their participation in exercises. Mexico is a partner in Exercise ARDENT SENTRY, our joint-field exercise focused on civil support and disaster assistance. Additionally, Exercise AMALGAM EAGLE was conceived around a coordinated U.S.-Mexico response to a simulated hijacking situation—similar to exercise VIGILANT EAGLE mentioned earlier.

### *The Bahamas*

The Royal Bahamas Defence Force is a trusted partner on our "third border" and our cooperative engagement with them continues to grow. The Bahamas provides a historic route for human smuggling and the smuggling of drugs and contraband into the U.S. due to its extensive size, small population, inadequate surveillance capability, and limited defense and police forces. This presents a pointed vulnerability to U.S. security and defense.

Our security cooperation efforts in The Bahamas are aimed specifically at better detection of human smuggling and the smuggling of drugs and contraband, improved communications interoperability, and increased disaster response capabilities. We recently completed air and maritime sensor deployments to the southern islands. These deployments confirmed the presence of illegal traffic flow through the Windward Passage. We secured funding for a permanent radar to assist with detection and tracking of suspect platforms in an effort to stem the flow of drugs, illegal migrants, and illicit materials. Our challenge is to prevent The Bahamas from returning to the TCO corridor it was in the 1980s and 1990s.

Due to the susceptibility of The Bahamas to natural disasters such as hurricanes and flooding, USNORTHCOM is collaborating with the National Emergency Management Agency of The Bahamas to enhance targeted disaster preparedness and response capacities. In December 2013, we completed construction and transferred possession of an Emergency Relief Warehouse to augment the warehouse previously donated by U.S. Southern Command. Additionally, we provided training and equipment to outfit the warehouses and enhance operational capacities. These facilities serve not only to assist our partner nation, but also to support the safety and security of the 35,000 American residents and more than five million U.S. tourists who visit The Bahamas annually.

### *Human Rights*

USNORTHCOM is committed to promoting an institutional culture of respect throughout the command and the AOR. Human rights considerations are factored into all our policies, plans, and activities and are an important component in our strategic engagement with partner nations and interagency relationships. The USNORTHCOM human rights program is working with partner nations to develop new programs of instruction on human rights, both in-country and at U.S.-based military education centers.

### *Western Hemisphere Institute for Security Cooperation (WHINSEC)*

Our regional engagement is enhanced by the efforts of WHINSEC, which continues to provide professional education and training to Latin America's future military leaders. The education offered by WHINSEC is a strategic tool for USNORTHCOM's international engagement, providing the most effective and enduring security partnering mechanism in the Department. Highlighting their commitment to the program, for the first time, Canada has detailed an instructor to WHINSEC.

### DEFENSE SUPPORT OF CIVIL AUTHORITIES (DSCA)

USNORTHCOM stands ready to respond to national security events and to provide support, as a DOD core task, to lead federal agencies for man-made or natural disasters. Our efforts focus on mitigating the effects of disasters through timely, safe, and effective operations in accordance with the National Response Framework. Although American communities display great resiliency in the face of tragedy, the scale of some events exceed the response capacity of local first responders and state and federal resources. Through an extensive network of liaison officers embedded in our headquarters and Defense Coordinating Officers throughout the U.S., we collaborate with interagency, inter-governmental, and non-governmental partners to plan and execute the rapid, agile, and effective employment of DOD supporting resources with a mantra of not being late to need. This includes our partnership with the Joint Improvised Explosive Device Defeat Organization whose capabilities and expertise are of great value to us and our interagency partners.

### *Dual-Status Commanders (DSCs)*

Last year USNORTHCOM continued to advance and refine the DSC program. Dual-Status Command is a military command arrangement to improve unity of effort with state and federal partners for DSCA missions. The Secretary of Defense, with consent of affected state governors, authorizes specially trained and certified senior military officers to serve in a federal and state status and in those separate capacities, command assigned federal and state military forces employed in support of civil authorities. In 2013, DSCs for Colorado's Black Forest fire and Front Range floods strengthened USNORTHCOM's close collaboration with the National Interagency Fire Center (NIFC), Federal Emergency Management Agency (FEMA), National Guard Bureau (NGB), and respective state National Guard Joint Force Headquarters. We continue to support the evolution and maturation of the DSC construct.

As part of the DSC Program, in collaboration with the NGB, USNORTHCOM conducts regular training for selected senior military officers through the Joint Task Force Commander Training Course and the DSC Orientation Course. We conduct state National Guard staff training and exercise programs through over 55 separate exercise events annually. Through 2013, we have trained and certified over 244 DSCs.

### *Council of Governors*

As a designated participant of the Council of Governors, I engaged in Council meetings this past year that helped advance important initiatives of the Council's "Unity of Effort" Action Plan, including continued development and implementation of the DSC command structure and development and sharing of support to civil authority shared situational awareness capabilities. I have also supported collaboration with the States, through the Council, on DOD's cyber force structure and a framework for State-Federal unity of effort on cybersecurity. USNORTHCOM and NORAD embrace the Council's initiatives throughout the year and incorporate them in operations, training and exercises, technical projects, and conferences. As an example, we recently hosted a conference on cyber challenges with The Adjutants General (TAGs) which provided a venue to better understand state and local cyber concerns and helped inform Service approaches to the future cyber force.

***Special Security Events***

We support the Department of Homeland Security (DHS) and the U.S. Secret Service (USSS) in the planning and execution of National Special Security Events (NSSEs). USNORTHCOM and NORAD partnered with USSS, Federal Bureau of Investigation (FBI), and FEMA to provide support to two NSSEs in 2013: the Presidential Inauguration and the State of the Union Address. Our support to the USSS and U.S. Capitol Police consisted of medical, communications, ceremonial, and Chemical, Biological, Radiological, Nuclear (CBRN) response forces.

USNORTHCOM and NORAD also assisted in several other high profile events. We partnered with the FBI, U.S. Immigration and Customs Enforcement, and FEMA for Super Bowl XLVII by providing aerospace warning and control, consequence management capability, CBRN planners, and liaison officers. We also coordinated with the West Virginia National Guard and Boy Scouts of America for the 2013 National Scout Jamboree by providing ground transportation, medical support, preventive medicine, and air traffic control. Lastly, we partnered with the USSS and Department of State to provide explosive ordnance disposal teams, explosive detector dog teams, aerial coverage, and communications for the United Nations General Assembly.

## CBRN Response Enterprise

The continued effort by terrorists to acquire and employ CBRN weapons in the homeland is well documented. The cumulative effects of globalization allow people and products to traverse the globe quickly, and the relative anonymity offered by the internet reduces technical obstacles to obtaining and developing CBRN terror weapons. In addition to a terrorist attack, we remain concerned for a domestic accident or anomaly involving CBRN materials.

USNORTHCOM continues to expand its relationships with NGB and whole-of-government partners to make significant strides in our ability to respond to a CBRN event by increasing the overall readiness of the nation's CBRN Response Enterprise. Though the enterprise is fully operational, USNORTHCOM continues to refine its requirements to achieve operational and fiscal efficiencies. Exercises are critical in this endeavor. VIBRANT RESPONSE is our joint exercise centering on training and confirmation of CBRN Enterprise forces. Last year's exercise, held at Camp Atterbury, Indiana, was a tremendous success, maximizing opportunities for tactical lifesaving integration and synchronization at all levels of local, state, and federal response.

## Wildland Firefighting

USNORTHCOM maintains the utmost readiness to support NIFC requests for suppression of wildfires that threaten lives and property throughout America. For over 40 years, as part of the national wildland firefighting (WFF) effort, DOD has provided support with C-130 aircraft equipped with the Modular Airborne Firefighting System (MAFFS) flown by the Air National Guard and U.S. Air Force Reserve. This past season, four C-130 airlift wings (three Guard and one Reserve) reinforced the national WFF effort through application of fire retardant on 46 federally mission-assigned fires.

When the Black Forest fire erupted less than 16 miles from USNORTHCOM and NORAD headquarters, we and a host of state and local partners, were well-prepared to meet the needs of our citizens. We maintained situational awareness as Fort Carson responded within two hours under Immediate Response Authority, as the Colorado National Guard engaged with helicopters and high-clearance trucks, tenders, and fire trucks. The 302nd Air Wing MAFFS quickly provided direct support from Peterson Air Force Base.

Later in the fire season, at the request of NIFC, we provided Incident Awareness and Assessment capability and MAFFS to the California Rim Fire, which threatened both the San Francisco critical power infrastructure and Yosemite National Park. Employment of a Remotely Piloted Aircraft (RPA) provided the unique capability to see through the fire's smoke plumes to improve command and control, as well as gain situational awareness on the fire's impact area. Use of the RPA demonstrated, with proper oversight, its outstanding capability to support a domestic scenario and showcased its potential to save lives and infrastructure.

### *Colorado Flood Response*

The 100-year flood of 2013 quickly tested the capacity of county and state resources in Colorado when rainfall inundated the Front Range, causing catastrophic flooding affecting 17 counties and resulting in disaster declarations in 14 counties. Helicopter crews from the Colorado National Guard, Wyoming National Guard, and 4th Infantry Division from Fort Carson, again acting in Immediate Response Authority, flew in difficult weather around the clock, working in parallel with ground teams to evacuate 3,233 civilians and 1,347 pets. The Colorado floods provided the first-ever opportunity to transition forces working under Immediate Response Authority by local commanders to a DSC for employment under a federal mission. This successful transition maintained unity of effort in accordance with the National Response

Framework and National Incident Management System. Alongside our federal, state, and National Guard mission partners, as well as the private sector, USNORTHCOM continues to develop and improve relationships enabling us to understand and rapidly respond to citizens in need.

### *Defense Support of Civil Authorities Playbooks*

An earthquake along the San Andreas fault, Cascadia Subduction zone, or New Madrid fault, just to name a few, could lead to a complex catastrophe that immediately becomes a national-level challenge. Hurricane Sandy gave us a glimpse of what impact such a catastrophe could have on our nation. So as not to be late to need, we are working with key stake holders (FEMA, NGB, and TAGs), in order to script likely initial response actions. I call these scripts "playbooks," and due to the maturity of the Southern California Catastrophic Earthquake Response Plan, USNORTHCOM is utilizing this scenario to develop the first one—with other states and regions to follow. This integrated response planning initiative will facilitate the most effective, unified, and rapid solutions; minimize the cascading effects of catastrophic incidents; and ultimately save lives.

## EMERGING MISSION AREAS/INITIATIVES

### *Special Operations Command North (SOCNORTH)*

SOCNORTH is a newly established Theater Special Operations Command (TSOC) aligned as a subordinate unified command of USNORTHCOM. This TSOC organizational alignment is consistent with existing constructs established in the other geographic combatant commands, with United States Special Operations Command (USSOCOM) retaining responsibility for manning, training, and equipping special operations forces. We aligned special operations activities throughout North America under a single commander, providing me with a flag officer who is operationally accountable for designated operations within our AOR. SOCNORTH also leverages USSOCOM's global network for partnerships and information collaboration in support of executing our homeland defense mission and enabling our partner nations. SOCNORTH operations conducted within the United States are in support of the appropriate federal agencies and in accordance with applicable laws and policy.

*Cyber*

Malicious cyber activity continues to be a serious and rapidly maturing threat to our national security. Over the past year, various actors targeted U.S. critical infrastructure, information systems, telecommunications systems, and financial institutions. As malicious cyber activities grow in sophistication and frequency, we believe an attack in the physical domain will be preceded by or coincident with cyber events. Of particular concern is the recent release of classified information.

The security breach of NSA intelligence not only created risk and enabled our adversaries in environments where forces are actively engaged in combat, it diverted attention to threat analysis and mitigation efforts which would otherwise be focused on protecting the homeland, which is ultimately the confluence and aim point of threat networks. This act informed our adversaries about risks and vulnerabilities in the U.S., and will almost certainly lead some of our most sophisticated and elusive adversaries to change their practices against us, minimizing our competitive advantage, and reducing the defense of not only the nation but also the approaches to the homeland. It also enabled the potential compromise of military capabilities and operations, further reducing the advantage held by our country. These breaches require us to acknowledge a potential vulnerability in the homeland, and question our operational security that underpins our planning and posture.

To integrate cyberspace operations for our commands and to foster an integrated operational cyberspace planning environment, we stood up a Joint Cyberspace Center. Within a year, we will begin receiving additional defensive capabilities to better protect our enterprise and missions. We are integrating defensive cyberspace operations into our concept plans, which will improve operational effectiveness and continue to increase the scope and scale of cyber play in our national-level exercises. We remain committed to strengthening our partnerships with key stakeholders—such as DHS, U.S. Strategic Command, U.S. Cyber Command, NSA, and the National Guard—demonstrated by our January 2014 Cyber TAG Conference.

**CONCLUSION**

Our nation depends on NORAD and USNORTHCOM to defend our homeland and cooperate with our partners to secure global interests. The security of our homeland is continually challenged by symmetric and asymmetric threats across all domains. Despite fiscal challenges, we must maintain our advantages and resiliency through enhancing international partnerships, providing Defense Support of Civil Authorities, and ensuring the defense of the nation and North America. The security of our citizens cannot be compromised. As the military reorganizes and reduces capacity and capability while confronting existing and emerging threats, I believe we must not "break" the things that give the military its competitive advantage: "jointness" to include training and exercises; the all-volunteer force; our national industrial capability; our time-trusted concept of defending the nation forward; and lastly our critical alliances and partnerships.

Threats facing our homeland are more diverse and less attributable than ever. Crises that originate as regional considerations elsewhere in the world can rapidly manifest themselves here at home. No combatant command operates in isolation; events outside the homeland have cascading effects on the security of North America and its approaches. The men and women of USNORTHCOM and NORAD remain diligent and undeterred as we stand watch over North America and deliver an extraordinary return on investment to the taxpayer. I am honored to serve as their commander and thank the committee for your support of this necessary investment in our national security. I look forward to your questions.

www.ingramcontent.com/pod-product-compliance
Lightning Source LLC
Chambersburg PA
CBHW080811290526
45790CB00008B/3660